Ice Mummies:
Frozen in Time

by Eric Kudalis

Consultant:

Arthur C. Aufderheide, M.D.

Department of Pathology and Laboratory Medicine

University of Minnesota, Duluth

CAPSTONE
HIGH-INTEREST
BOOKS

an imprint of Capstone Press
Mankato, Minnesota

Capstone High-Interest Books are published by Capstone Press
151 Good Counsel Drive, P.O. Box 669, Mankato, Minnesota 56002
http://www.capstone-press.com

Library of Congress Cataloging-in-Publication Data
Kudalis, Eric, 1960–
    Ice mummies: frozen in time/by Eric Kudalis.
    p. cm.—(Mummies)
    Summary: Describes ice mummies, how they are formed, some of the most
famous ice mummies, where they were found, how scientists study them, and what
they can teach us about the past.
    Includes bibliographical references and index.
    ISBN 0-7368-1307-1 (hardcover)
    1. Ice mummies—Juvenile literature. 2. Ötzi (Ice mummy)—Juvenile literature.
[1. Ice mummies. 2. Ötzi (Ice mummy) 3. Mummies.] I. Title. II. Series.
GN293 .K83 2003
599.9—dc21   2001007934

Editorial Credits
Carrie Braulick, editor; Karen Risch, product planning editor; Kia Adams, designer;
    Jo Miller, photo researcher

Photo Credits
AFP/CORBIS, 4
AP Photo/Martin Mejia, 6; Sergei Karpukhin, 16; Augustin Ochsenreiter, 20;
    El Tribuno, Osvaldo Stigliano, 26; South Tyrol Museum of Archaeology, 29
Charles & Josette Lenars/CORBIS, 18
CORBIS SYGMA, 10
Doug Wilson/CORBIS, 12
Reuters NewMedia Inc./CORBIS, cover, 28
Stock Montage, Inc., 23
VIENNA REPORT AGENCY/CORBIS SYGMA, 24
Werner Forman/CORBIS, 14, 15

Table of Contents

Chapter 1

A Mountain Discovery 5

Chapter 2

How Ice Forms Mummies 11

Chapter 3

Ice Mummy Secrets Revealed 19

Chapter 4

Ice Mummy Mysteries 27

Features

Map 8

Words to Know 30

To Learn More 31

Places of Interest 31

Internet Sites 32

Index 32

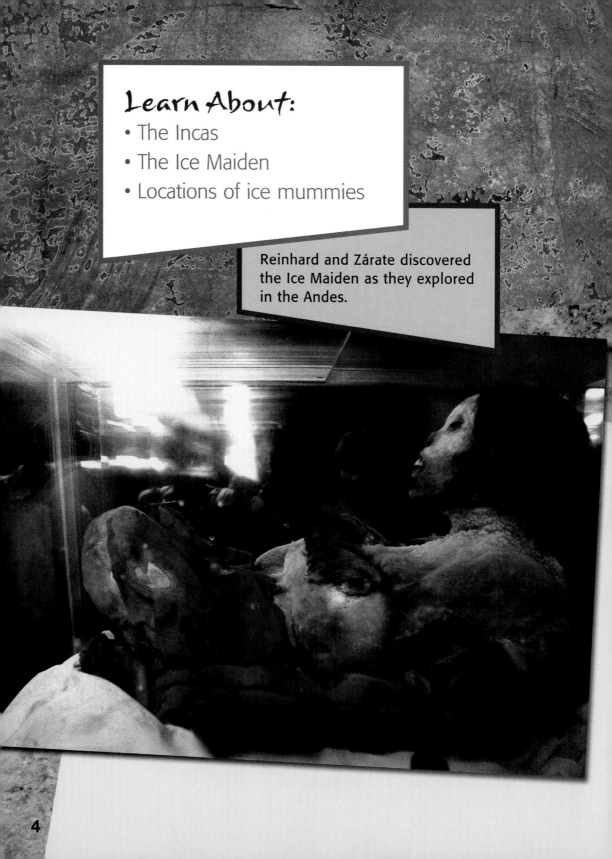

Learn About:
- The Incas
- The Ice Maiden
- Locations of ice mummies

Reinhard and Zárate discovered the Ice Maiden as they explored in the Andes.

Chapter One

A Mountain Discovery

In September 1995, scientist Johan Reinhard and his assistant Miguel Zárate were climbing Mount Ampato in the Andes. This mountain range is located in western South America. The two explorers were nearly 20,000 feet (6,100 meters) above sea level.

Reinhard was looking for remains of ancient Incan ceremonial sites. The Incas lived between about A.D. 1200 and 1532. Their empire stretched more than 2,500 miles (4,000 kilometers) along the Andes from Colombia to central Chile.

Scientists believe the Incas sacrificed the Ice Maiden.

Reinhard hoped to find pottery, jewelry, and sculptures. The Incas often held ceremonies in the mountains to honor their gods. He believed some ancient artifacts would be preserved in the cold conditions.

Reinhard's belief was correct. In 1990, the Sabancaya volcano began to erupt regularly. Ash from the eruptions dusted nearby Mount Ampato. The hot ash caused snow and ice to melt. Ancient artifacts underneath the snow then were revealed.

On September 8, the men discovered a bundle in a small clearing. They approached the bundle and saw a face. It was a child mummy that had been frozen for centuries.

Scientists named the mummy the Ice Maiden. They believe the Incas killed the child as a sacrifice to the gods. The Ice Maiden is one of the best-preserved Incan sacrifices ever found.

A Safe Arrival

Johan Reinhard carried the Ice Maiden down Mount Ampato strapped to his backpack. She weighed nearly 90 pounds (41 kilograms) frozen in the ice block. He traveled quickly to prevent the ice from melting.

At a base camp, Reinhard and Zárate loaded the mummy onto a donkey to take her to Cobanaconde, Peru. Reinhard then transported her in a bus to a laboratory in Arequipa, Peru. The Ice Maiden arrived frozen and undamaged.

Other Ice Mummies

Scientists and explorers have discovered ice mummies in other cold regions of the world. These places include Alaska, Greenland, and Russia.

In 1991, hikers discovered a mummy in the Alps. This mountain range is located in south-central Europe. Scientists named the mummy the Iceman. They believe the Iceman lived during the Neolithic period. This prehistoric period existed about 6000 to 2000 B.C.

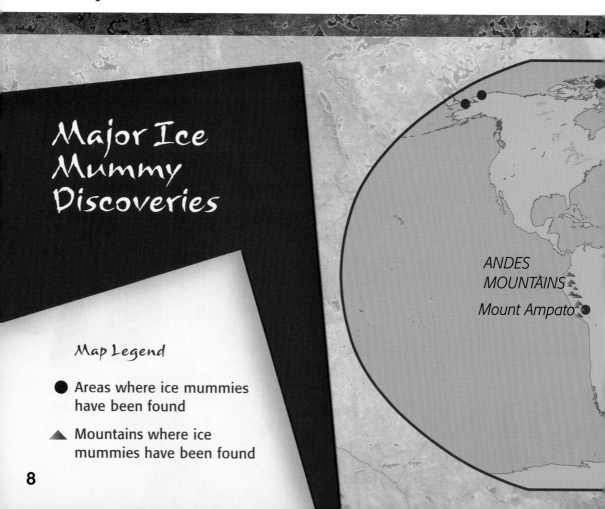

Major Ice Mummy Discoveries

ANDES
MOUNTAINS
Mount Ampato

Map Legend

● Areas where ice mummies have been found

▲ Mountains where ice mummies have been found

In 1845, Sir John Franklin and his crew sailed from England to North America. They were searching for the Northwest Passage. This waterway links the Atlantic and Pacific Oceans off North America's northern coast.

The crew found the Northwest Passage. But all 129 crew members died. Most bodies were never found. But search teams discovered three shallow graves on Beechey Island in 1984. This island is part of Nunavut in northern Canada. The ice had preserved the crew members' bodies.

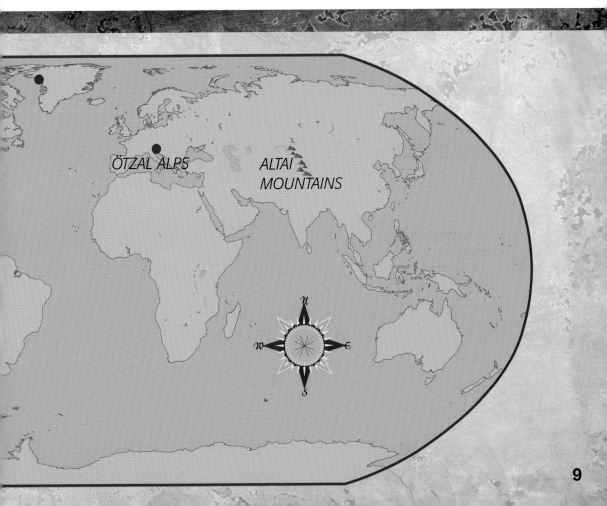

ÖTZAL ALPS

ALTAI MOUNTAINS

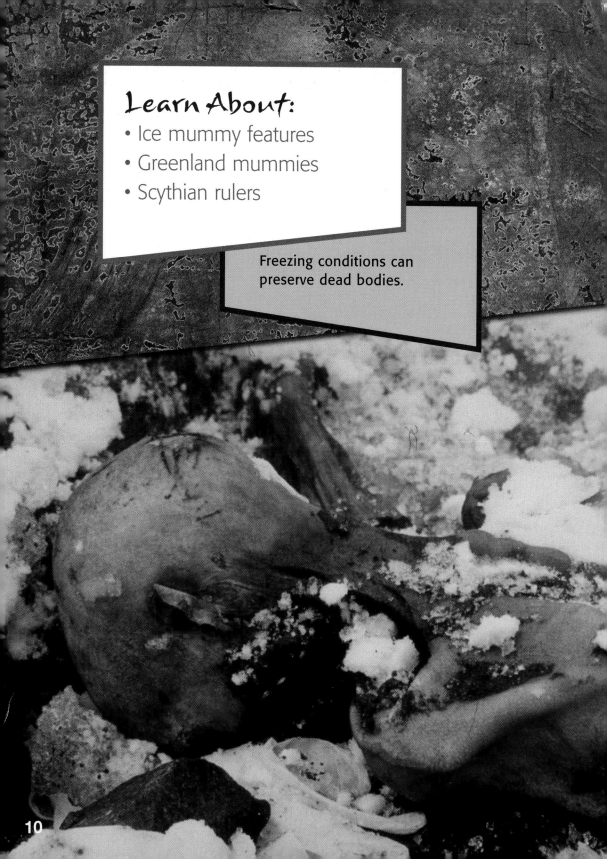

Learn About:
- Ice mummy features
- Greenland mummies
- Scythian rulers

Freezing conditions can preserve dead bodies.

Chapter Two

How Ice Forms Mummies

All living things decay after death. Small organisms called bacteria and fungi eat a dead body's tissues. The tissues break down until only a skeleton remains. But bacteria and fungi cannot grow in freezing conditions. A body that freezes solid soon after death can become a mummy.

An ice mummy has preserved tissues. The skin often remains on an ice mummy. A mummy also may have organs such as the heart, liver, and lungs.

Arctic homes often are located in remote areas.

Icy Conditions

Certain conditions must exist for an ice mummy to form. The temperature must stay below 32 degrees Fahrenheit (0 degrees Celsius). The body needs protection from weather conditions such as wind. The body also needs shelter so that animals do not eat it.

Few ice mummies have been discovered throughout the world. The polar regions have the coldest climates in the world. But the ground often is frozen too hard for deep graves. Animals and weather conditions then can destroy the bodies. Bacteria and fungi can grow as temperatures rise during summer.

Arctic Disaster

The region that surrounds the North Pole is called the Arctic. Arctic winters are long and dark. People often live in small family groups in remote areas. Few people are nearby when an emergency occurs. Some ice mummies form after people die in natural disasters.

In October 1972, three hunters found a woman's body on St. Lawrence Island. This island is near Alaska. Scientists believe the woman died when a large amount of snow and ice slid down a hillside near her home. The avalanche buried her house. Scientists believe the mummy is nearly 1,600 years old. She is the oldest Arctic mummy ever found.

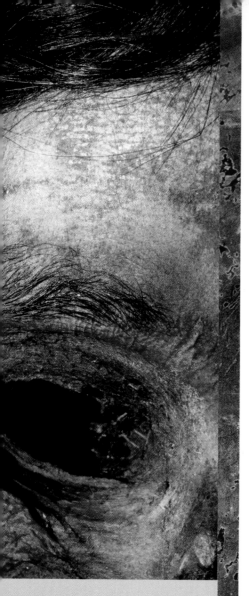

Lined tattoos decorate the area above the eyes on this Inuit mummy. Five of the six female mummies discovered in Greenland had similar tattoos.

Alaskan Mummies

Scientists believe other people who became mummies were victims of natural disasters. In 1980, a college research team discovered the remains of five family members in northern Alaska.

Scientists believe a violent storm shattered ice on the Arctic Ocean about 450 years ago. Strong winds blew the ice toward the family's house. The ice crushed and buried the family. Three bodies decayed to skeletons. But two bodies became ice mummies.

Greenland Mummies

In 1972, hunters discovered two child mummies and six female adult ice mummies in northwestern Greenland.

Scientists believe they were Inuits. This group of people lives in northern Canada, Alaska,

This child mummy was discovered in northwestern Greenland in 1972.

Greenland, and eastern Siberia. Scientists believe the people died in the late 1400s.

The surrounding conditions caused the bodies to mummify. Their environment had freezing temperatures. The bodies were located beneath rocks under an overhang. They were protected from rain, snow, and animals.

Russian Mummies

The Scythians lived in southern Russia more than 2,000 years ago. These people were nomads. They moved from place to place to find food instead of having a settled home.

Some Scythian rulers were preserved in the cold conditions of the Altai Mountains. The Scythians buried their rulers after they died. They placed the bodies in deep graves lined with wood

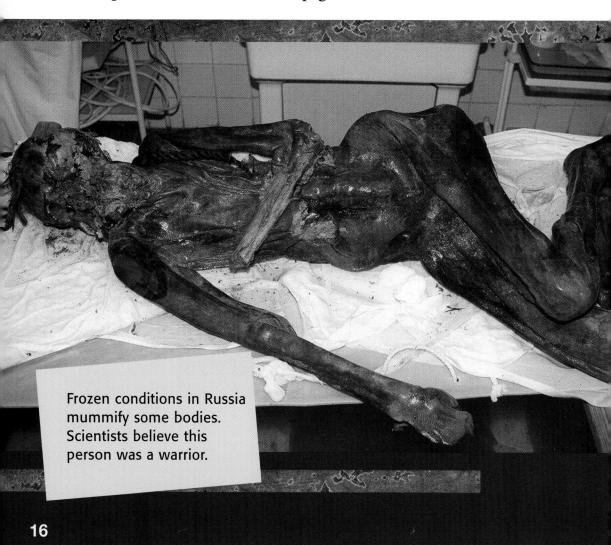

Frozen conditions in Russia mummify some bodies. Scientists believe this person was a warrior.

and rocks. They covered the graves with dirt. Cracks formed in the lining of some graves. Water seeped into the cracks. The water then froze and turned the bodies into ice mummies.

Incan Sacrifices

The Incas worshiped mountain gods and sun gods. They traveled high in the mountains to hold ceremonies. They believed sacrificing children at these ceremonies pleased the gods.

Explorers have discovered more than 115 ceremonial sites in the Andes. They found human remains from four Incan sacrifices on Mount Ampato. In 1999, Johan Reinhard discovered three well-preserved Incan sacrificial mummies on Mount Llullaillaco. Even the clothes on these child ice mummies were preserved.

Methods of Sacrifice

Scientists believe the Incas used several methods to kill their human sacrifices. Evidence suggests some victims were strangled. Clues also suggest the Incas sometimes broke the victim's neck or buried the person alive. Other times, they may have left the victim to die in the cold.

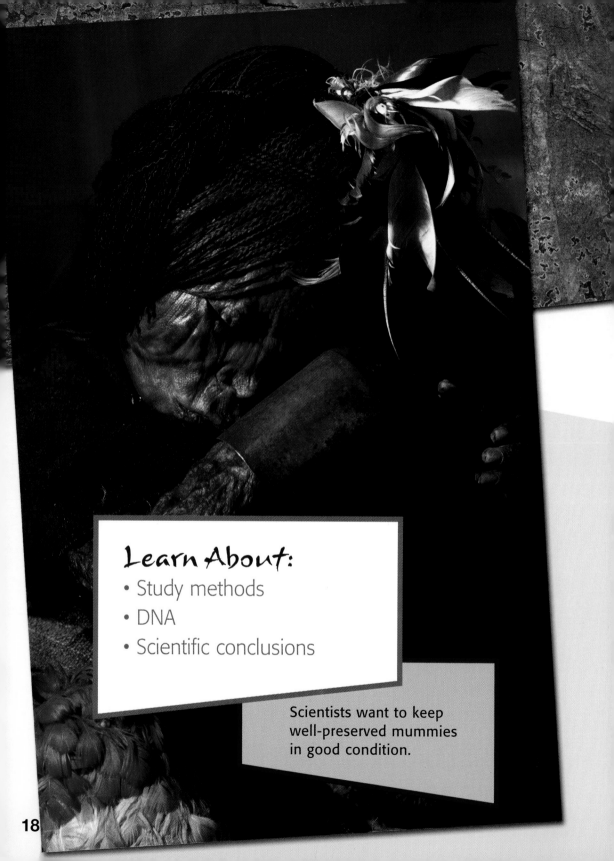

Learn About:

- Study methods
- DNA
- Scientific conclusions

Scientists want to keep well-preserved mummies in good condition.

Chapter Three

Ice Mummy Secrets Revealed

Scientists study mummies to learn about how people lived in the past. They try to use methods that will prevent damage to the mummies. They want to preserve the mummies for as long as possible.

X-rays and CT Scans

Scientists use x-ray machines to take internal pictures of ice mummies. The machines allow scientists to view a mummy's bones and internal organs without cutting it open.

Scientists also use CT scans. CT scans are similar to x-rays. But x-rays only show a flat view. CT scans allow scientists to see internal views from more than one angle at the same time.

DNA

Scientists may use DNA samples to study mummies. DNA exists in the cells of all organisms. It determines a person's physical features.

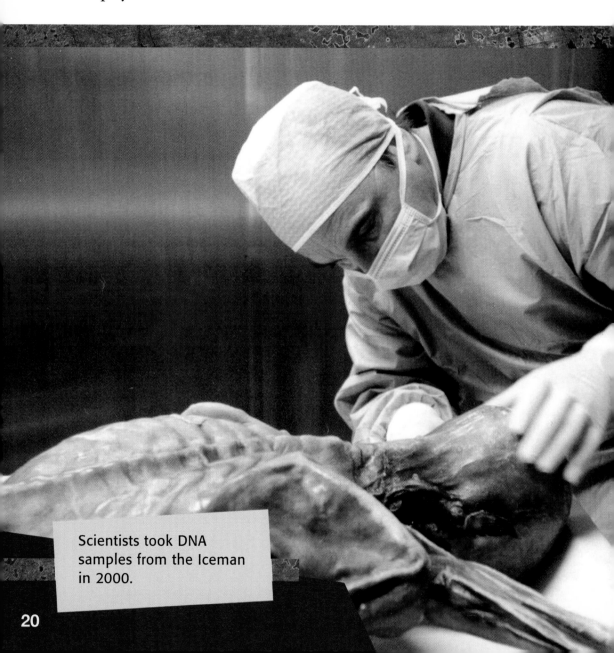

Scientists took DNA samples from the Iceman in 2000.

DNA tests can help scientists learn about a person's heritage. They may be able to discover if the person has any living relatives.

Endoscopes

Scientists sometimes use endoscopes to study mummies. They often insert these long tubes into a mummy's chest or stomach.

The tubes have a small camera that allows scientists to look inside the body. They may be able to see inside the intestines to learn about the person's diet. They also may be able to discover if the person had any diseases.

Radiocarbon Dating

Scientists use radiocarbon dating to learn a mummy's age. Radiocarbon called carbon 14 is found in all organisms. The element slowly breaks down after the organism's death.

Scientists measure the amount of carbon 14 a mummy contains. They believe mummies with little carbon 14 are oldest.

Examining the Franklin Mummies

In the 1980s, researcher Owen Beattie examined the three buried sailors from the Franklin voyage. In 1984, Beattie and his team of workers examined one body. In 1986, Beattie returned to Beechey Island to examine the other two bodies.

The researchers made a temporary laboratory on the island. They took tissue samples from the mummies and x-rayed them. Researchers discovered the three men had suffered from a lung disease called tuberculosis. They had empty stomachs and each weighed less than 100 pounds (45 kilograms).

The researchers also performed autopsies on the mummified sailors. They removed and examined the mummies' internal organs. The autopsies revealed that the bodies contained a great deal of lead. This soft, gray element is found in soil. Large amounts of lead can kill people.

Researchers studied tin cans found near the graves. The sailors had used these cans to store food. Scientists believe the material used to seal the cans contained lead. The lead then seeped into the food. They believe most sailors on Franklin's voyage died from lead poisoning.

Many search teams looked for remains of the Franklin expedition. But few bodies were discovered besides the three ice mummies.

Many scientists believe the Iceman suffered from painful bone joints.

Examining the Ice Maiden

In May 1996, scientists at Johns Hopkins University Hospital in Baltimore studied the Ice Maiden. The scientists used a hair sample to test for carbon 14. The test showed that the Ice Maiden is about 500 years old.

Researchers also took CT scans of the Ice Maiden. They noticed a crack in the Ice Maiden's skull near her left eye. Some scientists believe someone hit her on the head. These scientists believe the blow was so forceful that it instantly killed her.

Examining the Iceman

Researchers at the University of Innsbruck in Austria studied the Iceman. The scientists took x-rays and CT scans. The Iceman had several broken ribs and had suffered from poor bone growth. A test for carbon 14 showed that the Iceman is about 5,300 years old.

In July 2001, scientists discovered an arrowhead in the Iceman's left shoulder. They believe the Iceman died after the wound caused a great deal of blood loss.

DNA Samples

Scientists were able to take large samples of the Ice Maiden's DNA. They believe the Ice Maiden is related to American Indians. Her DNA patterns also were similar to the DNA of people in Taiwan and Korea.

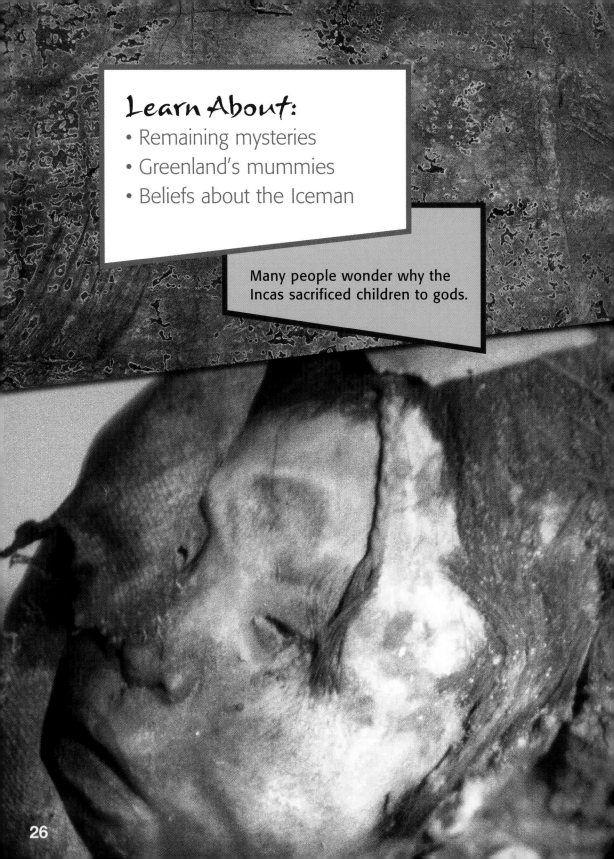

Learn About:

- Remaining mysteries
- Greenland's mummies
- Beliefs about the Iceman

Many people wonder why the Incas sacrificed children to gods.

Chapter Four

Ice Mummy Mysteries

Mysteries about several ice mummies remain. Many people wonder why the Incas sacrificed children to gods. The Spanish conquered the Incan empire in the 1530s. The Incas never developed any form of writing. Scientists must use the discovered sacrificial sites to learn about Incan culture.

Greenland Mysteries

Mysteries remain about the eight ice mummies found in northwestern Greenland. Several of these mummies were badly decayed. The decayed bodies were difficult for scientists to examine.

Frozen ancient artifacts can help scientists learn about ice mummies. This pouch and hand tool were found with human remains in Canada.

Researchers do not know whether the Greenland mummies died at the same time. They also are uncertain whether they died from the same cause.

Profiling the Iceman

Many people wonder why the Iceman was in the Alps. Researchers found two grains of barley in his clothing. They also found wheat plants in his pouch. Scientists believe he may have been a farmer.

Scientists found a variety of artifacts with the Iceman. The objects include an ax, a bow, a wooden backpack frame, and parts of two bark containers. These artifacts lead some scientists to believe the Iceman regularly traveled in the mountains.

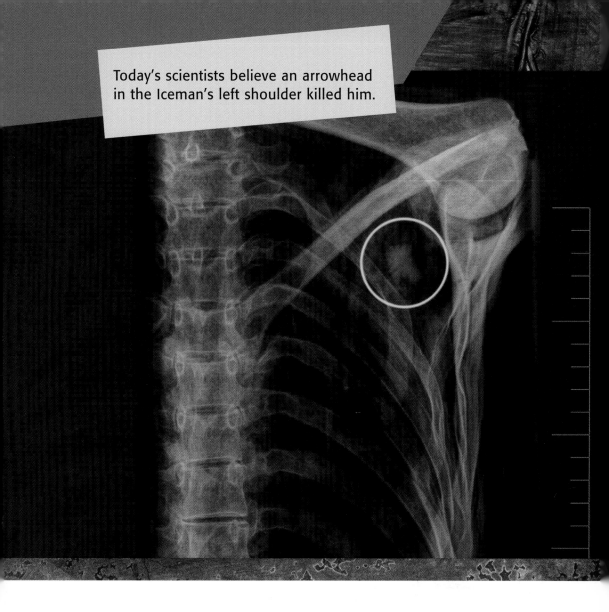

Today's scientists believe an arrowhead in the Iceman's left shoulder killed him.

No one will fully understand the events leading to the Iceman's death. But his body and artifacts remain the most complete record of the Neolithic period scientists have.

Words to Know

artifact (ART-uh-fakt)—an object used in the past that was made by people

bacteria (bak-TIHR-ee-uh)—very small organisms; bacteria eat the soft tissue of dead bodies.

fungi (FUHN-jye)—a type of organism that has no leaves, flowers, or roots

lead (LED)—a soft, gray element

parasite (PA-ruh-site)—a small organism that lives on or inside a person or animal

radiocarbon (ray-dee-oh-KAR-buhn)—a type of carbon that breaks down over time

sacrifice (SAK-ruh-fisse)—an offering made to a god

x-ray machine (EKS-ray muh-SHEEN)—a machine that takes pictures of the inside of a body

To Learn More

Buell, Janet. *Ice Maiden of the Andes.* Time Travelers. New York: Twenty-First Century Books, 1997.

Patent, Dorothy Hinshaw. *Secrets of the Ice Man.* Frozen in Time. New York: Benchmark Books, 1998.

Wilcox, Charlotte. *Mummies, Bones, and Body Parts.* Minneapolis: Carolrhoda Books, 2000.

Places of Interest

Greenland National Museum
Hans Egedevej 8
P.O. Box 145
DK-3900 Nuuk
Greenland
The Inuit mummies discovered in northwestern Greenland are located here.

National Museum of Natural History
Smithsonian Institution
10th Street and Constitution Avenue NW
Washington, DC 20560

University of Alaska Museum
907 Yukon Drive
Fairbanks, AK 99775-6960

Internet Sites

Ice Treasures of the Inca
http://www.nationalgeographic.com/mummy/index.html

The Mountain Institute—The Ice Maiden of Mt. Ampato
http://www.mountain.org/icemaiden.html

NOVA Online—Ice Mummies
http://www.pbs.org/wgbh/nova/icemummies

Index

Alaska, 8, 13, 14
Arctic, 13
artifacts, 6, 7, 28, 29

Beechey Island, 9, 22

carbon 14, 21, 24, 25
CT scan, 19, 25

DNA, 20–21, 25

endoscope, 21

Franklin mummies, 9, 22

Greenland, 8, 14–15, 27–28

Ice Maiden, 7, 24–25
Iceman, 8, 25, 28–29
Incas, 5–7, 17, 27
Inuits, 14

Mount Ampato, 5, 7, 17
Mount Llullaillaco, 17

Reinhard, Johan, 5–7, 17

Scythians, 16–17

Zárate, Miguel, 5, 7